Sermon, Lecture, & Bible Study Notes

2 Timothy 2:15King James Version (KJV)
15 Study to shew thyself approved unto God, a workman that needeth not to be ashamed, rightly dividing the word of truth.

This workbook belongs to:

Name _____

Email Address _____

If loss or found please return to owner:

(Sermon, Lecture, & Bible Study Notes)
Copyright © 2015 by (Jeru Publications)
www.jerupublications.webs.com
RE: Victoria Sheffield – Chain Breaking Ministries
Email: sheffieldvictoria39@gmail.com

If you enjoyed reading this book please give it a star review on Amazon.
ISBN-13: **978-0692585788** ISBN-10: **0692585788**

Printed in USA

Date: _____ Speaker's Name _____

Name of Church/Facility _____

Subject Title _____   Subject Subtitle _____

Scriptures _____   _____   _____   _____

_____   _____   _____   _____

Key Points:

_____

_____

_____

_____

_____

Notes:

_____

_____

_____

_____

_____

_____

_____

_____

_____

_____

_____

_____

Date: _____ Speaker's Name _____

Name of Church/Facility _____

Subject Title _____   Subject Subtitle _____

Scriptures _____   _____   _____   _____

_____   _____   _____   _____

Key Points:

_____

_____

_____

_____

_____

Notes:

_____

_____

_____

_____

_____

_____

_____

_____

_____

_____

_____

_____

Date: _____ Speaker's Name _____

Name of Church/Facility _____

Subject Title _____   Subject Subtitle _____

Scriptures _____ _____ _____ _____

_____ _____ _____ _____

Key Points:

_____
_____
_____
_____
_____

Notes:

_____
_____
_____
_____
_____
_____
_____
_____
_____
_____
_____
_____

Date: _____ Speaker's Name _____

Name of Church/Facility _____

Subject Title _____   Subject Subtitle _____

Scriptures _____ _____ _____ _____

_____ _____ _____ _____

Key Points:

_____

_____

_____

_____

_____

Notes:

_____

_____

_____

_____

_____

_____

_____

_____

_____

_____

_____

_____

_____

Date: _____ Speaker's Name _____

Name of Church/Facility _____

Subject Title _____ Subject Subtitle _____

Scriptures _____ _____ _____ _____

_____ _____ _____ _____

Key Points:

_____

_____

_____

_____

_____

Notes:

_____

_____

_____

_____

_____

_____

_____

_____

_____

_____

_____

_____

Date: _____ Speaker's Name _____

Name of Church/Facility _____

Subject Title _____   Subject Subtitle _____

Scriptures _____ _____ _____ _____

_____ _____ _____ _____

Key Points:

_____
_____
_____
_____
_____

Notes:

_____
_____
_____
_____
_____
_____
_____
_____
_____
_____
_____
_____

Date: _____ Speaker's Name _____

Name of Church/Facility _____

Subject Title _____   Subject Subtitle _____

Scriptures _____   _____   _____   _____

_____   _____   _____   _____

Key Points:

_____

_____

_____

_____

_____

Notes:

_____

_____

_____

_____

_____

_____

_____

_____

_____

_____

_____

_____

Date: _____ Speaker's Name _____

Name of Church/Facility _____

Subject Title _____   Subject Subtitle _____

Scriptures _____   _____   _____   _____

_____   _____   _____   _____

Key Points:

_____
_____
_____
_____
_____

Notes:

_____
_____
_____
_____
_____
_____
_____
_____
_____
_____
_____
_____

Date: _____ Speaker's Name _____

Name of Church/Facility _____

Subject Title _____   Subject Subtitle _____

Scriptures _____   _____   _____   _____

_____   _____   _____   _____

Key Points:

_____

_____

_____

_____

_____

Notes:

_____

_____

_____

_____

_____

_____

_____

_____

_____

_____

_____

_____

Date: _____ Speaker's Name _____

Name of Church/Facility _____

Subject Title _____   Subject Subtitle _____

Scriptures _____   _____   _____   _____

_____   _____   _____   _____

Key Points:

_____

_____

_____

_____

_____

Notes:

_____

_____

_____

_____

_____

_____

_____

_____

_____

_____

_____

_____

_____

Date: _____ Speaker's Name _____

Name of Church/Facility _____

Subject Title _____ Subject Subtitle _____

Scriptures _____ _____ _____ _____

_____ _____ _____ _____

Key Points:

_____
_____
_____
_____
_____

Notes:

_____
_____
_____
_____
_____
_____
_____
_____
_____
_____
_____

Date: _____ Speaker's Name _____

Name of Church/Facility _____

Subject Title _____   Subject Subtitle _____

Scriptures _____   _____   _____   _____

_____   _____   _____   _____

Key Points:

_____

_____

_____

_____

_____

Notes:

_____

_____

_____

_____

_____

_____

_____

_____

_____

_____

_____

_____

Date: _____ Speaker's Name _____

Name of Church/Facility _____

Subject Title _____   Subject Subtitle _____

Scriptures _____   _____   _____   _____

_____   _____   _____   _____

Key Points:

_____

_____

_____

_____

_____

Notes:

_____

_____

_____

_____

_____

_____

_____

_____

_____

_____

_____

_____

_____

Date: _____ Speaker's Name _____

Name of Church/Facility _____

Subject Title _____   Subject Subtitle _____

Scriptures _____   _____   _____   _____

_____   _____   _____   _____

Key Points:

_____

_____

_____

_____

_____

Notes:

_____

_____

_____

_____

_____

_____

_____

_____

_____

_____

_____

_____

_____

Date: _____ Speaker's Name _____

Name of Church/Facility _____

Subject Title _____   Subject Subtitle _____

Scriptures _____   _____   _____   _____

_____   _____   _____   _____

Key Points:

_____
_____
_____
_____
_____

Notes:

_____
_____
_____
_____
_____
_____
_____
_____
_____
_____
_____
_____

Date: _____ Speaker's Name _____

Name of Church/Facility _____

Subject Title _____   Subject Subtitle _____

Scriptures _____   _____   _____   _____

_____   _____   _____   _____

Key Points:

_____

_____

_____

_____

_____

Notes:

_____

_____

_____

_____

_____

_____

_____

_____

_____

_____

_____

Date: _____ Speaker's Name _____

Name of Church/Facility _____

Subject Title _____   Subject Subtitle _____

Scriptures _____   _____   _____   _____

_____   _____   _____   _____

Key Points:

_____

_____

_____

_____

_____

Notes:

_____

_____

_____

_____

_____

_____

_____

_____

_____

_____

_____

_____

Date: _____ Speaker's Name _____

Name of Church/Facility _____

Subject Title _____ Subject Subtitle _____

Scriptures _____ _____ _____ _____

_____ _____ _____ _____

Key Points:

_____

_____

_____

_____

_____

Notes:

_____

_____

_____

_____

_____

_____

_____

_____

_____

_____

_____

_____

Date: _____ Speaker's Name _____

Name of Church/Facility _____

Subject Title _____   Subject Subtitle _____

Scriptures _____   _____   _____   _____

_____   _____   _____   _____

Key Points:

_____

_____

_____

_____

_____

Notes:

_____

_____

_____

_____

_____

_____

_____

_____

_____

_____

_____

Date: _____ Speaker's Name _____

Name of Church/Facility _____

Subject Title _____   Subject Subtitle _____

Scriptures _____   _____   _____   _____

_____   _____   _____   _____

Key Points:

_____

_____

_____

_____

_____

Notes:

_____

_____

_____

_____

_____

_____

_____

_____

_____

_____

_____

_____

Date: _____ Speaker's Name _____

Name of Church/Facility _____

Subject Title _____   Subject Subtitle _____

Scriptures _____   _____   _____   _____

_____   _____   _____   _____

Key Points:

_____

_____

_____

_____

_____

Notes:

_____

_____

_____

_____

_____

_____

_____

_____

_____

_____

_____

_____

Date: _____ Speaker's Name _____

Name of Church/Facility _____

Subject Title _____   Subject Subtitle _____

Scriptures _____ _____ _____ _____

_____ _____ _____ _____

Key Points:

_____

_____

_____

_____

_____

Notes:

_____

_____

_____

_____

_____

_____

_____

_____

_____

_____

_____

_____

_____

Date: _____ Speaker's Name _____

Name of Church/Facility _____

Subject Title _____   Subject Subtitle _____

Scriptures _____   _____   _____   _____

_____   _____   _____   _____

Key Points:

_____

_____

_____

_____

_____

Notes:

_____

_____

_____

_____

_____

_____

_____

_____

_____

_____

_____

Date: _____ Speaker's Name _____

Name of Church/Facility _____

Subject Title _____   Subject Subtitle _____

Scriptures _____ _____ _____ _____

_____ _____ _____ _____

Key Points:

_____
_____
_____
_____
_____

Notes:

_____
_____
_____
_____
_____
_____
_____
_____
_____
_____
_____
_____

Date: _____ Speaker's Name _____

Name of Church/Facility _____

Subject Title _____ Subject Subtitle _____

Scriptures _____ _____ _____ _____

_____ _____ _____ _____

Key Points:

_____
_____
_____
_____
_____

Notes:

_____
_____
_____
_____
_____
_____
_____
_____
_____
_____
_____
_____

Date: _____ Speaker's Name _____

Name of Church/Facility _____

Subject Title _____   Subject Subtitle _____

Scriptures _____   _____   _____   _____

_____   _____   _____   _____

Key Points:

_____
_____
_____
_____
_____

Notes:

_____
_____
_____
_____
_____
_____
_____
_____
_____
_____
_____
_____
_____

Date: _____ Speaker's Name _____

Name of Church/Facility _____

Subject Title _____ Subject Subtitle _____

Scriptures _____ _____ _____ _____

_____ _____ _____ _____

Key Points:

_____

_____

_____

_____

_____

Notes:

_____

_____

_____

_____

_____

_____

_____

_____

_____

_____

_____

_____

Date: _____ Speaker's Name _____

Name of Church/Facility _____

Subject Title _____   Subject Subtitle _____

Scriptures _____   _____   _____   _____

_____   _____   _____   _____

Key Points:

_____
_____
_____
_____
_____

Notes:

_____
_____
_____
_____
_____
_____
_____
_____
_____
_____
_____
_____

Date: _____ Speaker's Name _____

Name of Church/Facility _____

Subject Title _____   Subject Subtitle _____

Scriptures _____   _____   _____   _____

_____   _____   _____   _____

Key Points:

_____

_____

_____

_____

_____

Notes:

_____

_____

_____

_____

_____

_____

_____

_____

_____

_____

_____

Date: _____ Speaker's Name _____

Name of Church/Facility _____

Subject Title _____   Subject Subtitle _____

Scriptures _____ _____ _____ _____

_____ _____ _____ _____

Key Points:

_____

_____

_____

_____

_____

Notes:

_____

_____

_____

_____

_____

_____

_____

_____

_____

_____

_____

_____

_____

Date: _____ Speaker's Name _____

Name of Church/Facility _____

Subject Title _____ Subject Subtitle _____

Scriptures _____ _____ _____ _____

_____ _____ _____ _____

Key Points:

_____
_____
_____
_____
_____

Notes:

_____
_____
_____
_____
_____
_____
_____
_____
_____
_____
_____
_____

Date: _____ Speaker's Name _____

Name of Church/Facility _____

Subject Title _____ Subject Subtitle _____

Scriptures _____ _____ _____ _____

_____ _____ _____ _____

Key Points:

_____

_____

_____

_____

_____

Notes:

_____

_____

_____

_____

_____

_____

_____

_____

_____

_____

_____

_____

Date: _____ Speaker's Name _____

Name of Church/Facility _____

Subject Title _____ Subject Subtitle _____

Scriptures _____ _____ _____ _____

_____ _____ _____ _____

Key Points:

_____

_____

_____

_____

_____

Notes:

_____

_____

_____

_____

_____

_____

_____

_____

_____

_____

_____

_____

Date: _____ Speaker's Name _____

Name of Church/Facility _____

Subject Title _____   Subject Subtitle _____

Scriptures _____ _____ _____ _____

_____ _____ _____ _____

Key Points:

_____

_____

_____

_____

_____

Notes:

_____

_____

_____

_____

_____

_____

_____

_____

_____

_____

_____

_____

Date: _____ Speaker's Name _____

Name of Church/Facility _____

Subject Title _____   Subject Subtitle _____

Scriptures _____   _____   _____   _____

_____   _____   _____   _____

Key Points:

_____

_____

_____

_____

_____

Notes:

_____

_____

_____

_____

_____

_____

_____

_____

_____

_____

_____

_____

Date: _____ Speaker's Name _____

Name of Church/Facility _____

Subject Title _____   Subject Subtitle _____

Scriptures _____ _____ _____ _____

_____ _____ _____ _____

Key Points:

_____

_____

_____

_____

_____

Notes:

_____

_____

_____

_____

_____

_____

_____

_____

_____

_____

_____

_____

_____

Date: _____ Speaker's Name _____

Name of Church/Facility _____

Subject Title _____   Subject Subtitle _____

Scriptures _____   _____   _____   _____

_____   _____   _____   _____

Key Points:

_____
_____
_____
_____
_____

Notes:

_____
_____
_____
_____
_____
_____
_____
_____
_____
_____
_____
_____

Date: _____ Speaker's Name _____

Name of Church/Facility _____

Subject Title _____   Subject Subtitle _____

Scriptures _____ _____ _____ _____

_____ _____ _____ _____

Key Points:

_____

_____

_____

_____

_____

Notes:

_____

_____

_____

_____

_____

_____

_____

_____

_____

_____

_____

_____

_____

Date: _____ Speaker's Name _____

Name of Church/Facility _____

Subject Title _____ Subject Subtitle _____

Scriptures _____ _____ _____ _____

_____ _____ _____ _____

Key Points:

_____

_____

_____

_____

_____

Notes:

_____

_____

_____

_____

_____

_____

_____

_____

_____

_____

_____

_____

Date: _____ Speaker's Name _____

Name of Church/Facility _____

Subject Title _____   Subject Subtitle _____

Scriptures _____   _____   _____   _____

_____   _____   _____   _____

Key Points:

_____

_____

_____

_____

_____

Notes:

_____

_____

_____

_____

_____

_____

_____

_____

_____

_____

_____

_____

Date: _____ Speaker's Name _____

Name of Church/Facility _____

Subject Title _____ Subject Subtitle _____

Scriptures _____ _____ _____ _____

_____ _____ _____ _____

Key Points:

_____
_____
_____
_____
_____

Notes:

_____
_____
_____
_____
_____
_____
_____
_____
_____
_____
_____
_____
_____

Date: _____ Speaker's Name _____

Name of Church/Facility _____

Subject Title _____   Subject Subtitle _____

Scriptures _____   _____   _____   _____

_____   _____   _____   _____

Key Points:

_____

_____

_____

_____

_____

Notes:

_____

_____

_____

_____

_____

_____

_____

_____

_____

_____

_____

_____

_____

Date: _____ Speaker's Name _____

Name of Church/Facility _____

Subject Title _____   Subject Subtitle _____

Scriptures _____   _____   _____   _____

_____   _____   _____   _____

Key Points:

_____
_____
_____
_____
_____

Notes:

_____
_____
_____
_____
_____
_____
_____
_____
_____
_____
_____
_____

Date: _____ Speaker's Name _____

Name of Church/Facility _____

Subject Title _____ Subject Subtitle _____

Scriptures _____ _____ _____ _____

_____ _____ _____ _____

Key Points:

_____

_____

_____

_____

_____

Notes:

_____

_____

_____

_____

_____

_____

_____

_____

_____

_____

_____

_____

Date: _____ Speaker's Name _____

Name of Church/Facility _____

Subject Title _____   Subject Subtitle _____

Scriptures _____   _____   _____   _____

_____   _____   _____   _____

Key Points:

_____

_____

_____

_____

_____

Notes:

_____

_____

_____

_____

_____

_____

_____

_____

_____

_____

_____

_____

Date: _____ Speaker's Name _____

Name of Church/Facility _____

Subject Title _____   Subject Subtitle _____

Scriptures _____   _____   _____   _____

_____   _____   _____   _____

Key Points:

_____

_____

_____

_____

_____

Notes:

_____

_____

_____

_____

_____

_____

_____

_____

_____

_____

_____

_____

Date: _____ Speaker's Name _____

Name of Church/Facility _____

Subject Title _____   Subject Subtitle _____

Scriptures _____   _____   _____   _____

_____   _____   _____   _____

Key Points:

_____
_____
_____
_____
_____

Notes:

_____
_____
_____
_____
_____
_____
_____
_____
_____
_____
_____
_____

Date: _____ Speaker's Name _____

Name of Church/Facility _____

Subject Title _____ Subject Subtitle _____

Scriptures _____ _____ _____ _____

_____ _____ _____ _____

Key Points:

_____

_____

_____

_____

_____

Notes:

_____

_____

_____

_____

_____

_____

_____

_____

_____

_____

_____

_____

_____

Date: _____ Speaker's Name _____

Name of Church/Facility _____

Subject Title _____   Subject Subtitle _____

Scriptures _____   _____   _____   _____

_____   _____   _____   _____

Key Points:

_____

_____

_____

_____

_____

Notes:

_____

_____

_____

_____

_____

_____

_____

_____

_____

_____

_____

Date: _____ Speaker's Name _____

Name of Church/Facility _____

Subject Title _____   Subject Subtitle _____

Scriptures _____   _____   _____   _____

_____   _____   _____   _____

Key Points:

_____

_____

_____

_____

_____

Notes:

_____

_____

_____

_____

_____

_____

_____

_____

_____

_____

_____

_____

Date: _____ Speaker's Name _____

Name of Church/Facility _____

Subject Title _____ Subject Subtitle _____

Scriptures _____ _____ _____ _____

_____ _____ _____ _____

Key Points:

_____

_____

_____

_____

_____

Notes:

_____

_____

_____

_____

_____

_____

_____

_____

_____

_____

_____

_____

Date: _____ Speaker's Name _____

Name of Church/Facility _____

Subject Title _____   Subject Subtitle _____

Scriptures _____   _____   _____   _____

_____   _____   _____   _____

Key Points:

_____
_____
_____
_____
_____

Notes:

_____
_____
_____
_____
_____
_____
_____
_____
_____
_____
_____
_____

Date: _____ Speaker's Name _____

Name of Church/Facility _____

Subject Title _____   Subject Subtitle _____

Scriptures _____   _____   _____   _____

_____   _____   _____   _____

Key Points:

_____

_____

_____

_____

_____

Notes:

_____

_____

_____

_____

_____

_____

_____

_____

_____

_____

_____

_____

_____

Date: _____ Speaker's Name _____

Name of Church/Facility _____

Subject Title _____   Subject Subtitle _____

Scriptures _____   _____   _____   _____

_____   _____   _____   _____

Key Points:

_____

_____

_____

_____

_____

Notes:

_____

_____

_____

_____

_____

_____

_____

_____

_____

_____

_____

_____

_____

Date: _____ Speaker's Name _____

Name of Church/Facility _____

Subject Title _____   Subject Subtitle _____

Scriptures _____   _____   _____   _____

_____   _____   _____   _____

Key Points:

_____

_____

_____

_____

_____

Notes:

_____

_____

_____

_____

_____

_____

_____

_____

_____

_____

_____

Date: _____ Speaker's Name _____

Name of Church/Facility _____

Subject Title _____ Subject Subtitle _____

Scriptures _____ _____ _____ _____

_____ _____ _____ _____

Key Points:

_____
_____
_____
_____
_____

Notes:

_____
_____
_____
_____
_____
_____
_____
_____
_____
_____
_____
_____
_____

Date: _____ Speaker's Name _____

Name of Church/Facility _____

Subject Title _____   Subject Subtitle _____

Scriptures _____   _____   _____   _____

_____   _____   _____   _____

Key Points:

_____

_____

_____

_____

_____

Notes:

_____

_____

_____

_____

_____

_____

_____

_____

_____

_____

_____

_____

Date: _____ Speaker's Name _____

Name of Church/Facility _____

Subject Title _____   Subject Subtitle _____

Scriptures _____   _____   _____   _____

_____   _____   _____   _____

Key Points:

_____
_____
_____
_____
_____

Notes:

_____
_____
_____
_____
_____
_____
_____
_____
_____
_____
_____
_____
_____

Date: _____ Speaker's Name _____

Name of Church/Facility _____

Subject Title _____   Subject Subtitle _____

Scriptures _____ _____ _____ _____

_____ _____ _____ _____

Key Points:

_____
_____
_____
_____
_____

Notes:

_____
_____
_____
_____
_____
_____
_____
_____
_____
_____
_____

Date: _____ Speaker's Name _____

Name of Church/Facility _____

Subject Title _____   Subject Subtitle _____

Scriptures _____   _____   _____   _____

_____   _____   _____   _____

Key Points:

_____

_____

_____

_____

_____

Notes:

_____

_____

_____

_____

_____

_____

_____

_____

_____

_____

_____

_____

Date: _____ Speaker's Name _____

Name of Church/Facility _____

Subject Title _____   Subject Subtitle _____

Scriptures _____   _____   _____   _____

_____   _____   _____   _____

Key Points:

_____

_____

_____

_____

_____

Notes:

_____

_____

_____

_____

_____

_____

_____

_____

_____

_____

_____

_____

Date: _____ Speaker's Name _____

Name of Church/Facility _____

Subject Title _____   Subject Subtitle _____

Scriptures _____   _____   _____   _____

_____   _____   _____   _____

Key Points:

_____
_____
_____
_____
_____

Notes:

_____
_____
_____
_____
_____
_____
_____
_____
_____
_____
_____
_____

Date: _____ Speaker's Name _____

Name of Church/Facility _____

Subject Title _____   Subject Subtitle _____

Scriptures _____   _____   _____   _____

_____   _____   _____   _____

Key Points:

_____
_____
_____
_____
_____

Notes:

_____
_____
_____
_____
_____
_____
_____
_____
_____
_____
_____

Date: _____ Speaker's Name _____

Name of Church/Facility _____

Subject Title _____   Subject Subtitle _____

Scriptures _____ _____ _____ _____

_____ _____ _____ _____

Key Points:

_____
_____
_____
_____
_____

Notes:

_____
_____
_____
_____
_____
_____
_____
_____
_____
_____
_____
_____

Date: _____ Speaker's Name _____

Name of Church/Facility _____

Subject Title _____   Subject Subtitle _____

Scriptures _____   _____   _____   _____

_____   _____   _____   _____

Key Points:

_____

_____

_____

_____

_____

Notes:

_____

_____

_____

_____

_____

_____

_____

_____

_____

_____

_____

_____

_____

Date: _____ Speaker's Name _____

Name of Church/Facility _____

Subject Title _____   Subject Subtitle _____

Scriptures _____ _____ _____ _____

_____ _____ _____ _____

Key Points:

_____
_____
_____
_____
_____

Notes:

_____
_____
_____
_____
_____
_____
_____
_____
_____
_____
_____
_____
_____

Date: _____ Speaker's Name _____

Name of Church/Facility _____

Subject Title _____   Subject Subtitle _____

Scriptures _____   _____   _____   _____

_____   _____   _____   _____

Key Points:

_____

_____

_____

_____

_____

Notes:

_____

_____

_____

_____

_____

_____

_____

_____

_____

_____

_____

Date: _____ Speaker's Name _____

Name of Church/Facility _____

Subject Title _____   Subject Subtitle _____

Scriptures _____ _____ _____ _____

_____ _____ _____ _____

Key Points:

_____

_____

_____

_____

_____

Notes:

_____

_____

_____

_____

_____

_____

_____

_____

_____

_____

_____

_____

Date: _____ Speaker's Name _____

Name of Church/Facility _____

Subject Title _____   Subject Subtitle _____

Scriptures _____   _____   _____   _____

_____   _____   _____   _____

Key Points:

_____

_____

_____

_____

_____

Notes:

_____

_____

_____

_____

_____

_____

_____

_____

_____

_____

_____

_____

_____

Date: _____ Speaker's Name _____

Name of Church/Facility _____

Subject Title _____   Subject Subtitle _____

Scriptures _____   _____   _____   _____

_____   _____   _____   _____

Key Points:

_____

_____

_____

_____

_____

_____

Notes:

_____

_____

_____

_____

_____

_____

_____

_____

_____

_____

_____

_____

Date: _____ Speaker's Name _____

Name of Church/Facility _____

Subject Title _____ Subject Subtitle _____

Scriptures _____ _____ _____ _____

_____ _____ _____ _____

Key Points:

_____
_____
_____
_____
_____

Notes:

_____
_____
_____
_____
_____
_____
_____
_____
_____
_____
_____
_____
_____

Date: _____ Speaker's Name _____

Name of Church/Facility _____

Subject Title _____   Subject Subtitle _____

Scriptures _____   _____   _____   _____

_____   _____   _____   _____

Key Points:

_____

_____

_____

_____

_____

Notes:

_____

_____

_____

_____

_____

_____

_____

_____

_____

_____

_____

_____

_____

Date: _____ Speaker's Name _____

Name of Church/Facility _____

Subject Title _____   Subject Subtitle _____

Scriptures _____ _____ _____ _____

_____ _____ _____ _____

Key Points:

_____

_____

_____

_____

_____

Notes:

_____

_____

_____

_____

_____

_____

_____

_____

_____

_____

_____

_____

Date: _____ Speaker's Name _____

Name of Church/Facility _____

Subject Title _____   Subject Subtitle _____

Scriptures _____   _____   _____   _____

_____   _____   _____   _____

Key Points:

_____
_____
_____
_____
_____

Notes:

_____
_____
_____
_____
_____
_____
_____
_____
_____
_____
_____
_____
_____

Date: _____ Speaker's Name _____

Name of Church/Facility _____

Subject Title _____   Subject Subtitle _____

Scriptures _____ _____ _____ _____

_____ _____ _____ _____

Key Points:

_____

_____

_____

_____

_____

Notes:

_____

_____

_____

_____

_____

_____

_____

_____

_____

_____

_____

Date: _____ Speaker's Name _____

Name of Church/Facility _____

Subject Title _____ Subject Subtitle _____

Scriptures _____ _____ _____ _____

_____ _____ _____ _____

Key Points:

_____
_____
_____
_____
_____

Notes:

_____
_____
_____
_____
_____
_____
_____
_____
_____
_____
_____
_____

Date: _____ Speaker's Name _____

Name of Church/Facility _____

Subject Title _____   Subject Subtitle _____

Scriptures _____   _____   _____   _____

_____   _____   _____   _____

Key Points:

_____

_____

_____

_____

_____

Notes:

_____

_____

_____

_____

_____

_____

_____

_____

_____

_____

_____

Date: _____ Speaker's Name _____

Name of Church/Facility _____

Subject Title _____   Subject Subtitle _____

Scriptures _____ _____ _____ _____

_____ _____ _____ _____

Key Points:

_____

_____

_____

_____

_____

Notes:

_____

_____

_____

_____

_____

_____

_____

_____

_____

_____

_____

_____

Date: _____ Speaker's Name _____

Name of Church/Facility _____

Subject Title _____   Subject Subtitle _____

Scriptures _____ _____ _____ _____

_____ _____ _____ _____

Key Points:

_____

_____

_____

_____

_____

Notes:

_____

_____

_____

_____

_____

_____

_____

_____

_____

_____

_____

_____

_____

Date: _____ Speaker's Name _____

Name of Church/Facility _____

Subject Title _____   Subject Subtitle _____

Scriptures _____ _____ _____ _____

_____ _____ _____ _____

Key Points:

_____
_____
_____
_____
_____

Notes:

_____
_____
_____
_____
_____
_____
_____
_____
_____
_____
_____
_____

Notes:

_____

_____

_____

_____

_____

_____

_____

_____

_____

_____

_____

_____

_____

_____

_____

_____

_____

_____

_____

_____

_____

_____

_____

_____

_____

_____

_____

_____

Notes:

_____

_____

_____

_____

_____

_____

_____

_____

_____

_____

_____

_____

_____

_____

_____

_____

_____

_____

_____

_____

_____

_____

_____

_____

_____

_____

2017

January
Su	Mo	Tu	We	Th	Fr	Sa
1	2	3	4	5	6	7
8	9	10	11	12	13	14
15	16	17	18	19	20	21
22	23	24	25	26	27	28
29	30	31				

February
Su	Mo	Tu	We	Th	Fr	Sa
			1	2	3	4
5	6	7	8	9	10	11
12	13	14	15	16	17	18
19	20	21	22	23	24	25
26	27	28				

March
Su	Mo	Tu	We	Th	Fr	Sa
			1	2	3	4
5	6	7	8	9	10	11
12	13	14	15	16	17	18
19	20	21	22	23	24	25
26	27	28	29	30	31	

April
Su	Mo	Tu	We	Th	Fr	Sa
						1
2	3	4	5	6	7	8
9	10	11	12	13	14	15
16	17	18	19	20	21	22
23	24	25	26	27	28	29
30						

May
Su	Mo	Tu	We	Th	Fr	Sa
	1	2	3	4	5	6
7	8	9	10	11	12	13
14	15	16	17	18	19	20
21	22	23	24	25	26	27
28	29	30	31			

June
Su	Mo	Tu	We	Th	Fr	Sa
				1	2	3
4	5	6	7	8	9	10
11	12	13	14	15	16	17
18	19	20	21	22	23	24
25	26	27	28	29	30	

July
Su	Mo	Tu	We	Th	Fr	Sa
						1
2	3	4	5	6	7	8
9	10	11	12	13	14	15
16	17	18	19	20	21	22
23	24	25	26	27	28	29
30	31					

August
Su	Mo	Tu	We	Th	Fr	Sa
		1	2	3	4	5
6	7	8	9	10	11	12
13	14	15	16	17	18	19
20	21	22	23	24	25	26
27	28	29	30	31		

September
Su	Mo	Tu	We	Th	Fr	Sa
					1	2
3	4	5	6	7	8	9
10	11	12	13	14	15	16
17	18	19	20	21	22	23
24	25	26	27	28	29	30

October
Su	Mo	Tu	We	Th	Fr	Sa
1	2	3	4	5	6	7
8	9	10	11	12	13	14
15	16	17	18	19	20	21
22	23	24	25	26	27	28
29	30	31				

November
Su	Mo	Tu	We	Th	Fr	Sa
			1	2	3	4
5	6	7	8	9	10	11
12	13	14	15	16	17	18
19	20	21	22	23	24	25
26	27	28	29	30		

December
Su	Mo	Tu	We	Th	Fr	Sa
					1	2
3	4	5	6	7	8	9
10	11	12	13	14	15	16
17	18	19	20	21	22	23
24	25	26	27	28	29	30
31						

2018

January
Su	Mo	Tu	We	Th	Fr	Sa
1	2	3	4	5	6	
7	8	9	10	11	12	13
14	15	16	17	18	19	20
21	22	23	24	25	26	27
28	29	30	31			

February
Su	Mo	Tu	We	Th	Fr	Sa
				1	2	3
4	5	6	7	8	9	10
11	12	13	14	15	16	17
18	19	20	21	22	23	24
25	26	27	28			

March
Su	Mo	Tu	We	Th	Fr	Sa
				1	2	3
4	5	6	7	8	9	10
11	12	13	14	15	16	17
18	19	20	21	22	23	24
25	26	27	28	29	30	31

April
Su	Mo	Tu	We	Th	Fr	Sa
1	2	3	4	5	6	7
8	9	10	11	12	13	14
15	16	17	18	19	20	21
22	23	24	25	26	27	28
29	30					

May
Su	Mo	Tu	We	Th	Fr	Sa
		1	2	3	4	5
6	7	8	9	10	11	12
13	14	15	16	17	18	19
20	21	22	23	24	25	26
27	28	29	30	31		

June
Su	Mo	Tu	We	Th	Fr	Sa
					1	2
3	4	5	6	7	8	9
10	11	12	13	14	15	16
17	18	19	20	21	22	23
24	25	26	27	28	29	30

July
Su	Mo	Tu	We	Th	Fr	Sa
1	2	3	4	5	6	7
8	9	10	11	12	13	14
15	16	17	18	19	20	21
22	23	24	25	26	27	28
29	30	31				

August
Su	Mo	Tu	We	Th	Fr	Sa
			1	2	3	4
5	6	7	8	9	10	11
12	13	14	15	16	17	18
19	20	21	22	23	24	25
26	27	28	29	30	31	

September
Su	Mo	Tu	We	Th	Fr	Sa
						1
2	3	4	5	6	7	8
9	10	11	12	13	14	15
16	17	18	19	20	21	22
23	24	25	26	27	28	29
30						

October
Su	Mo	Tu	We	Th	Fr	Sa
	1	2	3	4	5	6
7	8	9	10	11	12	13
14	15	16	17	18	19	20
21	22	23	24	25	26	27
28	29	30	31			

November
Su	Mo	Tu	We	Th	Fr	Sa
				1	2	3
4	5	6	7	8	9	10
11	12	13	14	15	16	17
18	19	20	21	22	23	24
25	26	27	28	29	30	

December
Su	Mo	Tu	We	Th	Fr	Sa
						1
2	3	4	5	6	7	8
9	10	11	12	13	14	15
16	17	18	19	20	21	22
23	24	25	26	27	28	29
30	31					

www.ingramcontent.com/pod-product-compliance
Lightning Source LLC
LaVergne TN
LVHW061336060426
835511LV00014B/1952